crawlspace

crawlspace

JOHN · PASS

HARBOUR PUBLISHING

Harbour Publishing
P.O. Box 219
Madeira Park, BC Canada V0N 2H0
www.harbourpublishing.com

Cover art by Paul Feiler b.1918, *Janicon LXXXIX*, 2004. Oil, gold leaf and gessoed
board on canvas, 71 x 71 cm. © Paul Feiler and the Redfern Gallery, London
Printed and bound in Canada

Harbour Publishing acknowledges financial support from the Government of
Canada through the Canada Book Fund and the Canada Council for the Arts,
and from the Province of British Columbia through the BC Arts Council and
the Book Publishing Tax Credit.

Library and Archives Canada Cataloguing in Publication

Pass, John, 1947–
        Crawlspace / John Pass.

Poems.
ISBN 978-1-55017-519-6

        I. Title.

PS8581.A77C73 2011   C811'.54   C2011-902427-6

In the gloom the gold
Gathers the light about it.
—*Ezra Pound*

CONTENTS

I. ENDLESS STREET

Mews	11
Mews 2	12
Mews 3	13
Endless Street	14
Trail & Medusa	15
As the Markets Fall	17
Off Bloor	21
On Elgin	23
Pennask Lake Road	25
Coeur d'Alene	26
Sparrows	29
En Route (Duncan Campbell Scott)	30
En Route	31
Fly-Ash	32
Destiny Itself	33

II. AKEBIA

Muse	37
Inch by Inch	38
WORLD	39
Inner Life	43
An Exact Understanding of It All	44
You Think	45
Around & Aboutist	46
Pine Beetle Transcription (Illustration: Ernie Kroeger)	48
Anthem	49
Birdbrain	50
A Warbler at My Window	52

muse 2   53
Que de beautez . . . (Pierre de Ronsard)   54
Beauty becoming . . .   55
A Four Word Title   56
Words   57
Parenting   58
Say No More   59
Twist   60
A Delicacy   61
Lost Thoughts   62
Repair   63
Janicon   64

III. SELF STORAGE
A View from the Lonsdale Quay Hotel   69
In the Corner of the Porthole   71
Pin-holes   72
Late Winter Rain   73
Bare Rock Relieved of Overburden   74
A New Footing   75
Late Matisse   77
Epic   79
Sitting With Tiger   80
Self Storage   82
Laszlo Loves Erasure   90
Finally   91
That May Be   92

Notes & Acknowledgements   94

I. ENDLESS STREET

We listen to what hidden longing for a mysterious street
is in us.

—*Mahmoud Darwish*

Mews

Warm wee pinkish pouch of need
this is your eyeless, clawless sound. This is your groping

voice in pre-world, into endless wherever. Singular seeker
of the mothering sweetness and milky, blooming light, you

are the first gear of universal
motion, seer from enclosure, perspective's

muscular origin, so I sing as I can
in your register, a little in remembrance, a little in fear.

Who hears us? Everyone
has this tear of your song within, lifelong. My mother

sobs its beginnings every moment moving
into her eighty-sixth year, in sigh/grunt small trapped

breaths of annoyance, frustration
that ache to cry for the opening dissolution,
the all-out terrible motherless wail

that is your destination.

Mews 2

A side to side quick thrashing

in the roadside brush on Hwy. 101, and then the bird above us
as if a pigeon struggled and flew, so plump and
pigeon-grey and pigeon-sized it was

but for the mouse it dangled. But for the drama of the backdrop light

against the startling substance of the clouds (mistaken
a moment for mountains) we were walking, of habit, home.
We had the mail. The hierarchy of hawks

in falconry allowed
a goshawk for the nobleman
and for the nun, this one, a merlin.
Enclosed in *mews* while *mewing* (changing
plumage) untamed, a bird, a world (and its oblivion)

is neither vast nor vague. It is an iron mist, a condensation
on the cage. And irony to float anew, aloft with rare precision
the strict, misplaced idea, the lost direction, a sacred scrap
of revelation re ferocity, fresh context for the glittering eye

and for the hood, the jesses, the training kite, the bells . . .
Dress, re-dress, amidst the mind's quaint heraldry, presides

to spin outside its threadbare ken
rehearsal for surprise.

Mews 3

In confinement stir great energies. Cyclical,
inevitable, a January née renaissance was restless
in the stalls. Stamping, steam from its haunches, flared
nostrils, it shouldered its way to the new boulevards, a coronation

coach in tow, a surf of cavalry its crown, and onto the battlefields
hauling the huge guns, where the sky came all the way down
to the ground. Artifact the skeletal cages, umbilical

lanes and vertical assumptions. Here we were choosing cleared space
and shocked air, the sea of banners in the square, the shattered cathedral.
Make way with a sun-struck confidence, processional flair.
We've hitched our wagons to this parade, each
one of us, each day in train. Along the upscale

thoroughfares, petite boutiques, belated cheers
for the homecomings. VE Day. Boxing Day. The retail chains
proclaim their blowouts. Duck into yonder cul-de-sac by that
little bistro for parking. These sprawled cities of the plain

beguile with antique niches still, their shell-casings of shelter.

Endless Street

In the place of the great cathedral
you can follow Blue Boar Row to

Market Square

to Endless Street, signposted (I kid
you not) on a handsome, windowed
wall like this:

Endless Street
Choices   *Choices*

Which options are delineated thus above
one door: *Movies   Games   Phones*

So go in there or otherwise pursue
three full blocks left the intriguing

endlessness that proves to be not going
on forever but a petering out

in bog once, now a built-up corner into
a new name: Belle Vue. So do go in or

left or past or right or
back the way you came. It's one. Or

follow me. Come on. Just turn the page.

Trail & Medusa

There's a good chance this first street leads somewhere
with its pioneer pedigree, that venerable North American history
of transition we used to call progress—from forest path
to wagon-road to freeway—and indeed it crosses
a quarter-mile isthmus, the land bridge Sechelt

rests upon. Its route from sea almost to sea, strait to inlet, and on
north suggests it may follow what was once a trail, tracking
the coast towards Skookumchuck, to drag beyond its first
just-visible, disappearing bend the promise
of destination, destiny even

imbedded in actual asphalt. But suspend your belief in Arrival here
at intersection with Old World complication, the Gorgon's gaze
(or just the look of her) that transforms idler and seeker alike

to stone, stymied. (And doesn't that mean while
still alive, with knowledge of the lost way forward, a horror
of writhing possibilities, conflicted purpose and fanged regret sprung
from her head?) From mine? My notion's poverty, its mere crossed

identifiers summon her almost gratefully onto the mundane
three blocks of suburbia (one east, two west) some town planner chose
for her in choosing her from his playbook of street names, sea-creatures.
A house across Medusa from me, a slope of dark cedars in the park kitty-

corner, another house across Trail: I worked twenty-two
years two blocks away and strode by carelessly thousands
of days, smiling at the irony. Behind me a patch of public garden
I could be standing in forever it feels so familiar but wow
no matter how famous I get don't ever let them

put my real permanent likeness there, in the cross–
hairs of a sparked mind's eye and drain–
swirl despair and wow again how did they (we!)

get it right somehow, at these arbitrary co–ordinates, on this
serendipitous ground, creating and peopling further back
on the lot of all things mythic or mortal
our log-cabin crucible:

an Arts Centre!

As the Markets Fall

As the markets fall I am talking beauty
at Eldercollege. Coming out from under

the ubiquitous sunsets and the eyes of the beholders
into September's last best weather, heading

for the lake to swim, I go down
the 959 points, dropping

in at the over-stuffed supermarket
for milk, lettuce, yogurt

and salmon contemplating Keats's
Truth becoming Emerson's, Dickinson's

(*scarce adjusted in the tomb*). Michelangelo's
purgation of superfluities. And can you believe Kafka:

Anyone who keeps the ability to see Beauty never grows old.
So who needs that pension plan to hold

its own? Ownership sets sail, sets
fire to the castle after all, catching

the dusk, unmoored on the tide of the beautiful day.

◻ ◻ ◻

As the markets fall I am hearing
Bayrakdarian's autumnal soprano
clasp and caress the burnished gold

and mahogany of the Armenian
repertoire, the yearning lullabies and love songs an over-
turned Muscat, an overture at our upper balcony.

To lamentation. Her countryman
beside my wife anticipates in breathless gasps and catching

sighs each finishing phrase. He is clapping over his head
and the friendly blonde of a certain age to my left is pressing

a little closer, proffering brass opera glasses
through which I can almost taste the diva's port wine

gown and the sheen of her shoulders. Outside
the streets are awash in a street lighting like moonlight

as we walk to our hotel where my wife has never been
more beautiful undressing and the phone message

from my financial advisor is the call I've already taken.

◻ ◻ ◻

As the markets fall I'm bucking up cedar, the rounds
off-round, cockeyed as my loud and dangerous
Homelite veers through each cut. I consider

getting a new saw but then what would I do
with this antique that runs well and could be
repaired, adjusted, taken better care of?

I would give it to the chainsaw museum
and miss this experience of a spread
bar and clumsy filing pulling

everything to the left every minute
I stand here on the bark shreds
trying to compensate, to wrestle

a winter's heat out of the weather
before the rain-heavy low sweeps in.

❑ ❑ ❑

As the markets fall I buy a new file
and insoles on sale for my old boots.
I think of investing in something
I really believe in, like wine (not

wineries, not wine futures, but a lot
of bottles) say, at one or so per day
for the rest of my life, 7300. Some
solace those mornings still feeling

for the bottom. Or *cheers* to a rebound!
Either way I'd be covered. I'm serious.
(So I buy a low interest GIC
instead.) There's nothing

much funny in a world financial crisis/correction;
after the election everything pulls to the right.

❑ ❑ ❑

As the markets rally like
a drowning body they don't
take long to sink again

but there are more cutthroat
trout in the small creek's spawning
channels this fall and the heavy rains

sustain them after holding off
while my brush pile burned
down to the charred stumps

of similar burnings in
past years. Everything
finds its level and the elemental

work goes on—a law
my advisor believes applies
to the markets. *That's why there are no*

1000 foot trees, is his buoyant assertion.
But its antithesis, the clear-cut,
is all too true: no forests

so proportioned greed won't gut them, gorge
upon them as upon its delusional numbers.

Off Bloor

What do I want of these cross-streets, side
streets that I have them in mind months later?
Those several shattered bicycles shackled
to chain-link, only their locks undamaged,
the stuffed panda tethered with coat-hanger
and bungie cord to the no-parking sign. A death
here commemorated? Someone run-over by someone

backing out of that driveway? A protest? What
was it upon waking in the B&B I wanted to savour,
celebrate? Not just the promise of spring on the main
drag, at bus-stops and under every over-hang

its thousands of butts emerging from the snow-banks. But
I woke up warming to that other Canada, my eastern, urban
heritage, the main-street cum suburban crowds and shabbiness
most of us live in now, the worst of Europe sans its Old World
glories of art, architecture. No-go apparently confronted

by the Korean restaurant, its window display a hand-
drawn map of the homeland(?) outlined in sorry
Christmas lights. No go where the old-school
entrepreneur founded Yorkville and opened
out everything west of Yonge. Even so next

to the city's best addresses I pressed on to offer (without
reservation) my *entire* country its due, generosity

in my heart and a skip in my step, on the cuff
of a rough wind in the empty elms rolling
into the streets the liberated beer cans from
the rolling garbage bins, on the spoor of flashes
of sun/heat off the handsome red brick duplexes,

via Westjet from my rural, coastal, paradisical West, I
had descended across the storied vastnesses (winter
on the prairies and all that) to encounter

a raccoon crossing Markham
I guessed for sure would be up an intervening
tree at my coming nearer, but which circled it keeping
between us our puny, groundling, companionable

distance as I passed mumbling aloud, bemused,
delighted, to the brown air:

There you are. Look at you. At home in the city.

On Elgin

The light is good on Elgin where it skirts
the canyons of high-rise convention hotels
and civil service offices. The light comes

low and bright outlining blocks and irregular
roof-lines. It floods intersections where my son
stands in silhouette kitty-corner as I've dropped

back to work the camera, to bask
in the sun's flashy flirtation with edges.

The light is good on Elgin
and the signs auspicious: DIGNITY
EGALITÉ Pure Gelato Perfect Books

Nothing is wanting on Elgin in its straightforward look
down the legacy of its namesake from Parliament Hill
to the overpass, the police station: responsible
government born of restraint, balance.

A father might follow his son on Elgin,
as is appropriate to time's shifts, reversals
in energy and power. *Where do you see yourself ten*

years hence I ask him, as fathers do knowing
there is no answer, no thought of the question
in one's twenties, no answer but apprehension
of the question in one's sixties. My impetus

wavers and wanes towards impotence at the tug
of the lovely young women on Elgin or passing
the loud young men near the pub. Even so

the signs are good: *buon appetito* Sugar Mountain
Our church has Aids. Walk with us.

Here is the neighbourly Mayflower Café sailing
almost allusion-free into the morning. Breakfast
and then, all day, the future! Though bearing

south (ever south!) the signs are benign on Elgin
and the light auspicious. Here it has cut a header

of shadow across the lettering under the bust
of General José de San Martin, liberator
of Argentina, leaving the honour and exploits

explicit, excising the name. The light is a sharp
wit with a chill chaser, a hiccup of spirit

worrying the surfaces. And there is some surface
(152 short years along, some layering to the mosaic)

to scratch at. The underfoot concrete's worn
through in places to red brick cobble,
and deeper to an older aggregate

and under that in the Hill's north face
and in the escarpment mid-stream
of islet in the Ottawa, broken shale

at the edge of the Shield. Upstream beside
the reconstructed native village the light
will be troubling the eddies reflecting

upon dissolution (ours) but holds close
and mostly grounded on Elgin to its literal

largesse: that in the accretion (depiction
and shadow) abides an elemental us.

Pennask Lake Road

It's not for the lake we take it, but its quick ascent
into golden light in the bunch grass and aspens, its top-
of-the-world openness in a coziness of gravelly bend and dip
and sharp shadow. Yes, we are incongruous, a few paces off

the shoulder with our new, smaller, blue cooler. Crackers and a sip
of wine among the cowpats and lumps of trampled, hardened clay.
On our way to dinner in the valley. You in your long black dress

are poised anywhere, but posed here
as if for a sixties album cover, whimsical incongruity.
My stance is anticipatory, arms at my sides not quite relaxed, mildly

anxious; will you follow my instructions
re the camera? Incongruous we are but only

marginally moreso than those redeemed
by significant purpose, first people

crouched low in skins, for example, hunting in the then high grass.
Or that rancher's pickup rattling past to Merritt for supplies.
Or even our younger selves intent back there at a tailgate
with kids and a picnic. Look both ways:

to the north steeply over
the near hills' sunny edges and up against further blue ranges, a glimpse
of Nicola lake; southwards a weathered barn below that ridge
of ponderosa forest. The long view's our forever

human incongruity in landscape, on earth. A given,
the distance. And a gift, to stretch us—restless reaches along the road.

Coeur d'Alene

When I mow the moss that passes
for grass here I wear my father's
last gift to me, pith helmet

molded of plastic straw sporting
a solar panel. When I step
into the sun a little

fan mounted in front of the hatband
blows air through a strip of wet sponge
at my brow. It's cool! It's working! When

I step into shade the breeze wanes
and ceases. When I mow the moss
that passes for lawn here I go back

and forth crossing the ground
in an orderly fashion and pattern my father
would approve of. Although there are patches

of low weed and rubble in no need
of mowing I mow them. I hold to the pattern.

◻ ◻ ◻

And when I mow here I go back and forth over
the first gifts he gave me: an electric train,
a jet plane sparking red in the tail

under friction, a two-tone peach-
and-green model convertible too delicate
to play with. My father was all about movement

and orderly process, goofy gadgets, a practicality
anxious, restless, virtually pointless. In short my father
was all about travel. My task when he went off

on business (sales and safety and
claims) was filling the tray in the forced air furnace
with water to the proper level, to maintain humidity. He went

to Great Falls. He went to Spokane. He met us gone camping
in Coeur d'Alene, where maybe he held me afloat as I learned
to swim, where we flew way up in a red flying boat, a lumbering

rattling contraption. The lake looked scuffed and yellow below
through the small scratched windows. Do I see now he went
to great lengths for me in his directions, and how in those

as in my own, as if they're my own, I've persisted, who was folded
once into his soft shoulder, into the shirt with the Lion's Club
crest, its cream-coloured rayon smelling of him, of summer?

◻ ◻ ◻

Fifty-five years later in Coeur d'Alene I'm guessing still
it took its name from some besotted *coureur de bois* far
from Québec and farther from France seeing

in the pretty lake his girl's face, or maybe her love
of wild, sweet places they lay together. It was whispered
my father had a girl in France before

my mother, before the war. We'll never know
with him departed, where his heart had journeyed. His heart
was (forgive me) another country, but one familiar, safe

enough and later took the cruise line, the tour bus, and took
photographs of every hotel lobby. Am I sure he was there with us
in Coeur d'Alene, *heart of the awl*, point of the awl, heart and point

of it all, perhaps? He loved dumb puns, but wouldn't
have gotten this one, and I confess I'm reaching for I know
not what via David Thompson's quirky name (in admiration, bitterness,

jest?) for the local Indians, after their sharp-point trading tactics, skill.
My father's gifts are with me, needling, working still, not lost. The moss
that passes for grass gets mowed. No pattern, no orderly pacing exactly

maps our story, connects the dots. In that, odds
are, I have him. And he has me.

Sparrows

On the lower concourse at YVR the lighting hangs
in swept-back wings of fluorescence above us, and sparrows

have got in somewhere through the glass expanses.
Trapped, they loop and weave their ways among the fixtures

in a magnified grace, with aerodynamic verve
and slide unseen in sparrows outside.

How they mock the stasis of our style, the stuckness
of the made thing, however edgy, and then prefer

the lit to light upon, as our light mocks
their dowdy, perching, ruffled dun—like little lumps

of clumsy animation in a hologram, blots on an HD screen.
And what is this, that one, with its thread of pink wool, wriggling

under the ill-fitted panel labeled CIRCUIT 6? An optimist?
A realist in our midst? Busy denizen, at home in our dark

densities, our nesting power, while we lean
back and crane our necks to gawk

awkwardly upward at the glare awaiting
the return of loved ones from the air, or flight ourselves.

En Route

The train has stopped for no apparent reason
In the wilds;
A frozen lake is level and fretted over
With rippled wind lines;
The sun is burning in the South; the season
Is winter trembling at a touch of spring.
A little hill with birches and a ring
Of cedars—all so still, so pure with snow—
It seems a tiny landscape in the moon.
Long wisps of shadow from the naked birches
Lie on the white in lines of cobweb-grey;
From the cedar roots the snow has shrunk away,
One almost hears it tinkle as it thaws.
Traces there are of wild things in the snow—
Partridge at play, tracks of the foxes' paws
That broke a path to sun them in the trees.
They're going fast where all impressions go
On a frail substance—images like these,
Vagaries the unconscious mind receives
From nowhere, and lets go to nothingness
With the lost flush of last year's autumn leaves.

—*Duncan Campbell Scott*

En Route

After take-off first the pinks, greens, tangerines
of Joliffe Island float-houses—struck match
eruptions of Yellowknife's upstart colours
against grey ice and black rock

where the Shield protrudes. Horizontal late sun

flashes off New Town's glass towers, off
 blo ts   ofmelt   on the strict ice-roads.

Then going fast where all impressions go
under the leading edge of wing, mist
and intimation, amorphous shadings
of lake in landform, all amoebic
limb and reaches

as if bruised spirit in the Barrens struggled
stranded in sepia but striking

as blood on snow. As if Kenojuak had a bear
or rabbit for us, sprawled. Glimpse and emblem

in our ascent, a heartbeat
hunting and hunted in emptiness—fully

lifted aloft in mammalian brain the dissolve
of journey's icon: animal. No pause, no rest

outside disaster. No nest nor root, but turbo-propped
to atmosphere thin sustenance: spin, thrust, thrum.

Fly-ash

The outdoor furniture and decks and roofs
are covered in fly-ash and dew.

Who'd be burning trash in the midst
of this heat-wave? Was there a bonfire

at the campground by the lake?
And then I remember the sirens last night

we assumed was an incident
at the park. Rowdies or a dive

into shallow water. I drive around
to find the fire's site, my neighbour's
log house burned to the ground. Lucky

there was no wind says the Chief, lucky
we've got this new reciprocal

agreement with the adjacent district.
With our one pumper we'd have been lucky

to stop this at the highway. Lucky.
My neighbour lost everything. Everything

went up in smoke and
sifted down through windless moonlight
to blanket a bigger everything: the surrounding hectares.

I've still got my view, he says.
I'm not leaving.

Destiny Itself

Yes it's best to settle things

with Sis, drink carrot juice, give thanks daily.
That's what we living do, persist

best in attentiveness. Take care
of business. But just as we showed up on time

here purposeless, empty-handed, shoeless,
in transit, flux, fluidity itself a-shimmer, destiny

itself netted
from the depths, at the reaches

of biology, culture, so
we will go out (on, wherever) that is, utterly

oceanic and unresolved.

II. AKEBIA

I sleep
with wet hair—in my dream
akebi vine

      —Akao Tooshi

    and

what we thought was clearest Mind really
  was that glancing girl, that
    swirl of birds . . .

      —Lew Welch

Muse

Here it is then, the unmade poem, enormous block
of stone slung overhead, invisibly yoked to heaven,
or there behind me, somehow

winched in, elephant monolith in the room. To whom
might I appeal? Lord of the Doom Burden? Lord
of the Slick Surface nonchalance, of loose change
tossed on the side table, sliding, of the greased skids,
of the black ice lacquer that spins one

twice and makes a beginning of ending
up, facing elsewhere? Skittering thought. His terrible clichés.
No forward way. And that ice-cube brain, the brittle thinking.

I have months of notes, schemata, that belie a liquid center, a scrambled
yolk, the yellow lines on asphalt,

saltings. On this first beautiful morning in weeks. Winds
for weeks and the now stilled

trees, those sentinel, whole and broken, erect in frosted
eminence. All in a sunlight that's got me pleading no
depths please, no context, pleading no contest . . .

only what's worked up into seeing, verdant
edge of virgin forest, shimmer of sea, verbose and splashy
where everything's evident, nothing known, a bird, a flutter

of light at my shoulder. O Lady of the Lost Ways I knew
locus, nexus, your street address, the musk of your sheets.
Now stone chisel, ice-pick, lug-wrench, hammer
for the melting moment.

Inch by Inch

You know you should be out in moonlight.
Every night the moonlight beckoning, even driving

to the book club caught sight of in the rear-view
mirror, shining on the highway behind where
your headlights don't. How are you that

figure not even at the window?
Dark figure shrouded standing, an inch
or two of moonlit floor at your feet

an inch or two of moonlit ground at your feet
in circumference you can't inch into.
Snow promised, holding off.

WORLD

the rest is silence

—William Shakespeare (*Hamlet*)

This is the most ambitious poem
ever. Whatever's thought and done

goes in. Even the future
translator wrestling *aspen*

into Mandarin. His ink.
His toenail clippings. Shale

and grasslands. Zephyr over
lake water, trembling

aspen. (You knew it was coming!) Maybe
that satellite crossing into Cassiopeia past

a new moon. Or cross it out if you care to.
Negation is included. Not being awake much

longer in the Quilchena Hotel, it's difficult
to think of everything but I'll leave room

at the end for the rest.
The End—what a thought . . . (

The Rest

Refreshment and remainder.
Or a simple pause, a guileless

silence undeniably dramatic
when acknowledged, heard

for what it is, where in the score
it's entered. It's none of my business

by definition but I won't
let it rest. A restless voice

puns, makes incursion, degradation
and revelation . . .

Makes reminder. A second glass
of wine at lunch escorts my glance

out the eatery window into a narrow
and elegantly balanced space framed

by columns of the porch: a blur therein
of salmony reflection on wet asphalt,

a tailfin of sedan, a snippet of string
of Xmas lights blinking along the eaves

of the gym opposite. Bland sky. I
could pedal the machine forever

of this paradisical digression, dangled
ever elselessness, as if living outside . . .

as if outside were other than extended
notation, potential incidentals, inevitable

links and lines to the luscious details
hauled, homing. As if beyond the baubles . . .

Therest

For most *there* choose a mode
of concentration. Intimate, oblivious

head on the pillow of the *h*, feet
to the foot's *t*, compromised

waywordly, pray for luxuriant
dream-life (surprise, surprise!)

or Newton's sleep even, sensible
assumption there's an object

in the room. There's an om
in room. And a moo. And a mr.

There's a being complicit in the error
of our making. He's thought to be

most present. Dream. Pray.
Reason. There you be, dear

reader, all. Imaginary. One,
with me, of our threesome.

There St.

Everyone came home
though somewhat delayed by snow.

He was looking forward to Christmas
before beginning treatment.

Having a keen sense of difference
and danger he couldn't be assimilated

but was moved by the exotic byways
in a foreign movie. Two friends died.

He had the means to go anywhere
but stayed put to take care

of the old dog and the hot-tub
which were outdoors.

One on an island, the other on a delta.
They went about as best they could

on the deep trails and along
the ploughed edges. The subtitles

were assimilated in the human interest.
To the day the melt began.

If you turn left here it will be
through a beaded curtain.

St. stands for saint as well.
There's no way in the world.

Inner Life

In the city of rosy stone and remnants
of rain it was decided so I descended

the escalator and the long corridor
to your friends and kin gathered
by the mound of bedding. Under

the white quilt and the largest upturned
ice-cream bucket you were sleeping in porcelain.
In Belleek, in its greeny white sheen

of mummy bag and bud of head, you were draped
slug-like over the lift of pillows, over the jam-
pot lid, a kind of handle. A miniature

lamenting snoring somewhere
between whistle and moan sounded
clear . . . muse   clear . . . muse when
through the glaze your eyes opened and time

enough to get to Canadian
Tire on the southside, if not
to make the hearing across the line
where the jury was hung

from its heels, hung around cooling
its heels, hung as soon for the almighty

dollar as for the dime. Turned spare there
and towards us was the torch of rose
you carried for Tom lain

aside beside you. Besides you
were wanting bolt upright and out
not down, were wanting

but found.

An Exact Understanding of It All

If you miss the point
don't worry. You can be sure

the point won't miss you.

You Think

Anything might goose-
step or side-step into mind to enthrall

one. A thrill, a pang, a blood-
pressure reading. You think

is this the first or last
straw, surrender

to the miniscule conflagration? As when
my mother became convinced
her house was toxic

in its furnace, in its heat-pump
and chimney, and wouldn't shut up about it

thereafter: chest pains and dry sinuses and almost
passing out. She wouldn't stay home

and at Emergency an inconclusive
hour or two, at my sister's place a recuperative
day or two, feeling better, she knew

it was the metal there also
in the baseboard heater, a virus,

or fumes from the raccoon she'd seen
in the garden she'd loved.

Around & Aboutist

At length to lean my chilly ears to this, faithless, wanting
the one thing I've had forever, babble a-bubble
to soothe and flow inward and onward, to circle and suckle

thinking in swath and swaddling, surprised in snow itself
to perambulate warmed and worshipful. At seventeen weaving
up Laurentian Crescent friend Nick said to me—in the thick of

a new moon's mercury, slaking my thirst on phrasing splashed

after rhyme, half-astride meaning, words bucked and bouncing at random
away on spilled pearls, swirling strings that left the right brain as moon-
struck and open as meditation— "you blathering Mercutio, you're

one can be drunk on nothing." So I'll listen now woken
in dark and brittle stickle, in merciless simplification, rigidity
for any old headlong in-hiding recitation, original mutter

and take it to heart as I knew to. Take it downstairs to stumble
around in the kitchen or up and down the mountain in the morning.
Time past is time too coming around. Reading yesterday

of A. S. Byatt's poet, Hugh Pink, in *Babel Tower*, walking
the Herefordshire countryside in '64, puzzling loosely o'er
the noose, obliquity, it was as I put the key in my parents'

backdoor in Coquitlam, silenced with care not to wake them
in their separate rooms, and tiptoed slowly the dim split-
level hallway. A century after Dickinson slanted

the difficult light. And still it is slanting and slipping poetry
about our heads. Unsettling lasso. Which once *whished* more
directly that the world was real, and the soul

and the like. And oh sweet remaining reader or two I want
to leave more in words than words can do, theoretically.
Adrift in our blether bedding, reunion, I want you

to have the shaggy grey-green scarf of leaf
about your ears, yes, even in darkest January
the leafiness extant and vague above the pergola

that never has to begin again, that never knows
the New Year but continuance only
and veracity, tenacity. *Akebia*

that even in its complex inter-lacings
with the white rose and snow light and tight air isn't
as Theresa notes, a strangler, so we should leave it be.

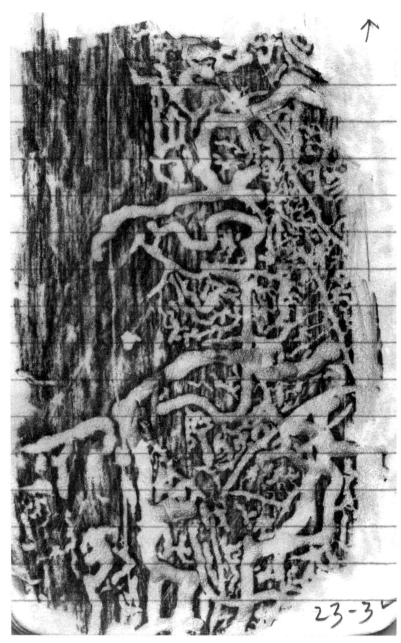

Pine Beetle Transcription

Ernie Kroeger

Anthem

We scrabble, we thrive
in exquisite dimension, excavate
sweet atmosphere, go with the phloem.

The Cold has gone, the killing Cold
retreats before us. Old from flutter over

golden grasses, we hone in, we dim, we hunger . . .

To translate the flesh of our apprehended
unknowable Lords, ascendencies, light
sifters, sky kin. To defy

their pollens, glade and shadow, siskin air, squirrel

banter, our expansionist gnawing articulates living-
room abandoned, unlivable, tongues out the liquid
contiguous letter

of our Constitution, miraculous archive. Pride!
Virginal vastnesses civilized each generation.
O endless essence. O embryo. O salamander.

O venturing left. O stranded dancers. O
fevered thinking, contusion dreams!

O grey from green
has there ever been
life on earth like ours?

Birdbrain

This carefree flock of chickadees might be
of one, albeit skittish, mind swooping
into the vegetable garden

then under feeders hung
on the clothesline, then up
the fir into ivy thicket, particular ones

within the swirl delayed or forerunning or choosing
opposing directions, a pop-corny joyous hopping substrate
of the larger purpose, if there is purpose, or thinking, or choosing

in what they do, or in my seeing. They have their grubs and seeds
to be sure, and I my automatic gear slipped into, pursuing
furtherance—so much of so many and such

tiny birds but when
last did art ask less

than everything of anything to hand, as if
there is ever enough to hand, really, anything much self-evident
of the true complexity, deep chickadee. Some take such little

flights they are more broad-jumps of a yard or two, and as I'm watching
them for that, what do the others do? Awake after midnight raking
the recollection I extrapolate vectors

and trajectories for their discrete, erratic
bursts of energy and see it must be everything between

the lines, outside the lines, I'm asking too: the sun in the trees, glossiness
of ivy leaves and smell of fresh-turned earth . . .
Again, a bare beginning

sub–atomic almost, or a heartbeat after as when
the smashed atom, particulate,

escapes the cyclotron. Does it? I know so little
and want so much from the tag-ends of thinking, tendrils
savaged in the scribbled ball of tracings where chaos, or semblance
or meaning began (begins, begins . . .) in the flock's cohesion.

A Warbler At My Window

April again, bright morning and he's back, flinging
senseless against the pane his scruffy plumage,
his shit and mucous and god knows what other
bird-body fluids . . .

He's at it as if a warbler's winter, the complicated stormy signals
of exhausting migration, the daily mastery of distance and direction
were unlived irrelevance next to this masculine frenzy: perpetual sexual
spring where a year passed, or sixty, brings neither solace nor wisdom.

The battered self bangs on unrecognized,
mistaken for rival, its harrying blurred riddle

flung back in our faces, the intimate, invisible boundaries
smutched endlessly up against. He pauses, and pants

into focus: blacks and whites and high-lit yellow,
a sharp eye on me from the sill. He's just torn apart
the bedroom, jerked off feebly on her lingerie
and a chill, a dislocation

sends him hopping and stopping, chest puffed, flustered
along the sundeck handrail, strut in a parallel world. His obsidian

chip of beak points at the sky, all arrogance's
puny arrowhead, and then

side-long surprise, release
on steep trajectories away, a slide
of gluttonous high-strung duende: song.

muse 2

read more says she in her white shift passing me

                              leaf   leaf   leaf   leaf   leaf
a sprig, a broken branch branch branch branch branch branch leaf
                    leaf   leaf   leaf   leaf   leaf

what can I do with this? plaintive, petulant, gruffly ahead I cast

it aside. it was

saskatoon maybe or ocean spray, smallish rough leaves serrated one
curled centrally reddish against its dark green edge

what can I do with this gimme text

Que de beautez . . .

Que de beautez, que de graces écloses
Dans le jardin de ce sein verdelet,
Enflent le rond de deux gazons de lait,
Où des Amours les fleches sont encloses!

Je me transforme en cent metamorphoses,
Quand je te voy, petit mont jumelet,
Ains du printemps un rosier nouvelet,
Qui le matin caresse de ses roses.

S'Europe avoit l'estomach aussi beau,
Sage tu pris le masque d'un toreau,
Bon Jupiter, pour traverser les ondes.

Le ciel n'est dit parfait pour sa grandeur,
Luy et le sein le sont pour leur rondeur:
Car le parfait consiste en choses rondes.

—Pierre de Ronsard

Beauty becoming . . .

Beauty becoming, the budding graces
swell your young breasts to a freshening fullness
in this milky pre-dawn light across dew-wet lawns
where Love takes her end to end archery practice—

I tremble, transfixed, transformed
glimpsing them, and their sister, your little mound,
new rosebush, that spring's aurora arouses in roses.

As Zeus, with a bull's grand certainty
took his Europa, lightly, over ocean and the vast
discreet undulations of her gorgeous belly

so the sky is not a perfection of distance
but of completion, of the sun's curve touching
upon roundness, arrival: your perfect breasts in full daylight.

A Four Word Title

Halfway back to the house on the lawn burnt off
in driest June since '35 (provoker

of the tasks, the cutting and dragging of ocean spray
from fire-prone slope far enough away hope-

fully to a brush pile out back)

my thought relaxes, sees side to side and towards my study
window's slatted venetian blinds that this is wholly

possible from the outside like encompassing daylight
or its slant on brickwork opposite the Victorian Hotel

I saw with relief for its deep information, its content turning
away from morning television (the news even) possible

with a dignified four word title beginning with D,
dream greenery gently impinging, a pillowed

confusion and forgetfulness such that I don't drive, saying
the same thing twice to my wife minutes apart, *aural-like*

mental phenomena on the ultrasound imaging requisition.
There is something to do that can never be that we

can't come to terms with not doing. We are all
the avant-garde I remember scribbling under

My Dinner For One at Al Porto attempt that finished with
Cointreau over ice and the homeless. Canada Place

in full sail past the rail-yard, edges ablaze with sunset.

Words

Words all night in my dreams unremembered except
in their hungry attachments, their grapplings and urgencies.

So morning knows it is theirs first and finds ways
and leans far out to them. Their long patience

throughout the weeks of carpentry and care-
taking will be rewarded. Their tolerance

of the red pen underlining *movement/moment*
or *spaciousness/us* will be rewarded. Their tolerances

be damned the rain is starting in all the false starts. The rain
is building to crescendo on the parched lawns and metal

roofs. In the trees and gravels and parentheses
of the world it is raucous and rivulet the words at last

in waves and saturate say everything not
under eaves. Even those things, a rake or deckchair

or a sad idea

feel the heave and sigh of the new air the freshening
of the words becoming themselves then everything then

evaporating.

Parenting

EEEEEEEYYYYYUUUUUUNNNNHHH

Use your words. Say
oops, I dropped my hat.

Don't go

EEEEEEEYYYYYUUUUUUNNNNHHH

Say No More

I've been walking, walking, walking,
walking. A marginal, distracted pacing though it traverse

mountain-sides, headlands. Though it show me
lakes and islands, elk and grouse and blackberries

and snakes on the trail, I've nothing to show
for it—am tirelessly, tiresomely, unequal to it. I've tried to name

the light for example because it's September and nothing
is finer now. A high, full moon all night on the 20th.

Clarity, and a gleam that deepens
the days, that has deepened in things and erased

their glare. Colours are become Venetian, especially
the rusts and clarets and russets. History in them.

And more. I begin to feel a little
sympathy, an almost excusable self-

pity declaiming, outpacing
the enormous stasis of my thought.

Twist

At a twist of flashy ribbon knotted
to the fence-wire months back

to spook seed-eaters
and the rose-hungry deer

the year's last hummingbird
needling after September essence.

A Delicacy

What holds me here, suspended
between the gutter-end and

empty air, the grunt work
and the perfect fit? I would say
it's a delicacy of touch, a feel

for preparation. I would say it
but the silicone caulking has smeared

on my fingers and on the new end-cap, askew—you holding
the ladder, me letting go with my other hand, my left,
of the top rung and reaching across myself

for the pliers in the right-hand pouch.

Lost Thoughts

Lost thoughts, return to me! Can you
pulse through my fingertips on the keys

with that frisson of confident beginning
I loved in you? That thread of connection.

Through and through, a stitching. Yes I can do
the present tense, the Snyder, the zen. But really,

didn't we know some worthy, sewn-up moments
of comprehensive reverie, of timeless

certainty before you bolted, amnesiac,
to soul's den is it? Is it there invisibly

you sift from the folds, the notes to self,
this dingy abstraction we're curled in?

In these close quarters . . . where the path
in sunlight leapfrogs up to me over

the gravels and shadowy distractions
you are lost to me. Where the far air condenses

to green fire in the firs and gold sheen on the maples
you are lost to me. Where perfectly at a middle-

distance we come to attention and words
are things and things words, there

too, right here, you are lost to me.
But are, and have been, mine to lose.

Repair

To make right even with the stitches
showing in the place of solace or
supposed escape, as in

*let us repair to the bridge and there
reconnoitre.* Or to the bedroom. Or coming back

with your doppelganger, your soul-mate, the party-goer
on your arm. I mean back

home to the party. I mean with
the one you took, who takes you, the one
you're taken for

and showing them (and showing them
off) and showing yourself
yourself. Beyond.

Janicon

Some images await one, a summing up.
Years in the studio, the collections, and then

that boisterously breezy day we entered
(in St. Ives escaping seascape, platoons of flashy

lively waves in sunshine and dive-
bombing gulls) the gallery, small rooms impossibly

containing Feiler's *Janicon* series. These hung
as burnished shield, moon-heavy window, trick

doorway. Place-settings at the god's
groaning board. Circle in rectangle endlessly

teasing. Absolute Geometry. Suns and Survey.
Mirror, umber, depth of field. Distance

at play with its transgressors.
Is there something, I scribbled down

parallel to do in language?
The catalogue quotes Whitman: *Darest thou now*

O soul / Walk out with me toward the unknown region . . .
The catalogue quotes Pound: *In the gloom the gold*

Gathers the light about it. I sit down
with my mother months later in her garden pergola.

I sit down with my mother outside in her last
moments at home, in her last moments before

the Home, the crazy talk a moment suspended.
A bird passes. I tell her many times after on the phone

how her wisteria has grown to command our patio . . .
the lattice filling, portals closing, shade. There is nothing

parallel to do in language. Do you see?
Do you see in the null shine how we're leaving

everything behind? I refer you to the catalogue.

III. SELF STORAGE

I founder in desire for things unfound.
I stay amid the things that will not stay.

—*Geoffrey Hill*

A View from the Lonsdale Quay Hotel

In the seams of grey on grey, sea under sea mist, propelling
the bobbing whites of pleasure boats and the colourless

push of the seabus toward vague cityscape, in the guts
of the engines and the sheen of the hulls (but nowhere

loudly declaring itself) twists ingenuity's filigree. (I have the craft exactly
on a shelf at home, Portuguese galleon souvenir, a gift from a girlfriend
decades ago, a good breeze bustling in the flags and rigging
delicately implied.) So hugely

intricate, fragile, the centuries of tinkering expended, required
to float this scene, this cargo, my reverie. To float it daily, worldwide.
To hold it taut and hardy as these hawsers hugging
tugs to the pier: the compendia

of knots and resins, of sorties and sea-trials, models in wood and clay.
Of screw styles, bulkhead design, torque and caulking.
Lubricants, hydraulics, sonar, radar. The casting
of brass. The story of rubber.

The chemistry of paint . . . and underhand suddenly, somehow
(exhausted in the listing, fretful, effervescent, disbelieving)
this miniscule, fervent, pushing-off again . . . my weight shifting

against the balcony railing—a richly enameled white the partially
                                              extended ferry rusting

in dry-dock adjacent could use . . . One door behind me I've left

open. Its pair is permanently screwed shut to the jamb. Venetian blinds
rigged cleverly inside the double-glazing, askew, cords snarled, broken,

can't be fixed now without taking apart the entire
contrivance. Won't be. Have to be
lived with, seen through. Apart

from me I discern, indistinctly, dully, one
living thing, one effortlessly lifting being. A gull.

In the Corner of the Porthole

Real life is continuous beyond one's wilful
plod and propellant instances: contiguous, sinuous
and undecided

in tide pools, slippery as old acquaintance against
pilings, the smoothed resistances. Voluminous chapter headings

in their little boxes (New Year's, Teen Swim, The Sahara: 6 pm . . .)
are dissolved or float superciliously off on errant currents, slid
in broad daylight from the freighters' holds. Glimpsed blind-

folded in the corner
of the porthole, impediment himself, dear cousin

walks the plank, all moony.

Pin-holes

My paired photo prints of Ankor Wat portals, deepening, extended
passageways, light slanting in through

jungle foliage, the stone blocks and columns worn, leaning,
laced with verdigris, red sand between the flagstones, a small blue

final upright rectangle in one's diminishment, the suggestion
of a human back and shoulders in the other's conclusive dark. These two

studies are the first for which I put
pin-holes in my study walls.

Late Winter Rain

Late winter rain stealthy at the south

eaves, then thunderous overhead.

This huge, too quiet house.

Bare Rock Relieved of Overburden

is essential landscape, all I need of absolute or hard
philosophy—scars of the backhoe's

bucket, my shovel scratches, as nothing
against its clunk, finality. Getting there is enlightenment.

Where charcoal chunks in the hardpan next to granite declare
original organics razed to the ground, to the very ground, there

I have it: steadfast calm. After the pressure-
washing, a sluice and stain of soil migrating

down shallow inclines, over plateaus and into minute ponds illumines
long-held secrets of the rain, seepages where the underarm muscle

and fingerlings of cedar root were suckled. Pebbles, new erratics, over-
night in their millennia in the scattering of fir needles gusts

have tossed across first morning's sun-struck plain.
And into crevices, just far enough
from where I stopped

working, thinking, fine sediment settling begins again.

A New Footing

I've had in my head some weeks the imaginary line
square-rule timber framers work from in a beam's heartwood
to assure true bearing, but busy myself with patches, surfaces
for a concrete footing under the living room's outer edge.

I've observed it eroding, crumbling for three years at least.
Renovation, that's the word for my sixties, keeping up

with things begun in my thirties as best I can. I construct
a plywood box 16 inches square around the old
12 inch diameter column. This will work

in theory, hold together with a facing
of sand and water and Portland cement

the disintegrating center.
But what I think most of once begun is not
the heavy mix shoveled in and leveled, nor

the abstractions that sustain us, the structures dreamed up
out of nearly nothing, from the inside out, for a life, a poem,
a clearing in the forest. Of the past-lives of smooth pebbles

shimmering in a creek-bed, washed
out of the old concrete into dusty light, new dusk,
I think only a little. And I'm cognizant merely a moment

or two of the other footings in the crawlspace gloom.
I won't examine them just yet. What's next

can wait. What I think of before, and during
and after my work, what I wake with glinting

in the nights while the new footing cures,
are the shiny screws, the yellow zinc # 6 screws I used
to join the plywood corners without splitting them. I think

of unscrewing those slender screws from the form.

Late Matisse

I have come from Late Matisse (his pleasing
pools and appliqués of colour, his shapely half–
blind joie de vivre) and too at ease meander
too far east in Sainte-Chapelle between

the non-identified apostles
with my glasses off

so the rose window a vortex seems
of spun tears, flung rain, constrained
within and splashed (especially
green) upon its ground. Apocalypse

contemporaine. Kaleidoscope
as threshing machine, haymaker.
Where worlds collide in early May

on Ile de la Cité, les boulevards, les quais, loosen
their belts between the bridges, replete

with arrival, contemplation. The centuries
of human movement beneath the seat
of administration, beneath

the Crown of Thorns and the once
revolving angel are slow processional, confluence
font to altar, nave-bound to the reliquary . . .

and then again are lightning instance, wink
of light in the jewel that is

petal and leaf (in glass and past
the glass) a perfection of Time, synapse

and collision of the world's end
and beginning, collusion of the world's end

and beginning over the heads of unidentified
beheaded martyrs and the quatrefoils depicting

other punishments
inflicted on martyrs
unidentified with certitude.

Epic

In tall air behind my future
there is light's crescendo, a jewel
of water, ornamental cherry. These

(and everything else) remain.
These in everything else remain un–

natural selection, this instant's
short–shortlist, estranged

from the full world (rattled
dice in a cup) adjacent to,
nudging each other, but

bereft of intimacy, bereft
of my epic, incidental bias.

Sitting With Tiger

Death's imminence is emanation, smudgy
edge or edgy whiff become an inward
sovereign ink, then atmosphere, her bad breath

heavy about us where I cradle her head,
squeeze water from a soaked sock along
her gum-line. Not fierce, ferocity

belongs to life entirely: the afternoon's heart-
lurching cramps and cries

exhausted, diminished to flinches
of her jaw, last lift of her ribcage
under my hand, barely

perceptible shudder chest to throat—
It's OK. It's OK. I look up
to see away, to see

the world as was, before this daze
and blur of the treetops. Who ever
could sit easily with her? See

this emailed jpg. from friends, a condolence
of us last summer perched on the same
porch, top of the stairs, her not posing, pulling

back under the crook of your arm, me glancing
at the photographer, smiling. You smiling
at the dog. *You'll have just a second*

to get this: her wary about-to-be
frantic eyes, ears and brow ruckled
forward under the drag of your headlock.

Escape! Always that unbalanced, goofy,
wildness to her. At our backs the closed
screen-door, the wide open

real door behind it, a corner of window
across the living-room, out the window

scant mass of murky foliage in daylight.

Self Storage

no ideas but in things . . .

—William Carlos Williams

Soul went.) So long going! For millennia
into the earth boxes, into pits and ditches,
pyramids. Onto pyres. Up trees. On water.

As breath, as smoke, an adjacent zephyr, defiant
in denial that disappearance wasn't, the gone not.

Went reverent, sentimental, wan
on the lips of Self Ascendent in America's

prophecy. Sidelined in Emerson's
reliance. Sump of Whitman's song.

Went slower than bone and flesh to ash, ponderous
with ceremony, incense and remembrance

to nothing (but nothingness its bread and butter!)
but went just the same, went marginal, clinging

to the food and music (stick to your ribs
grits, earthy sorrow) of the dispossessed.

Not once found a way but in a body.
Not once found a way out, wandered

into a mist in the wings, a drawn dawn
or a chalice lifted on sonorous

mumbo-jumbo. Went lower-case, adjectival 'til
gone and good riddance, nudged along

by its woollier substitute teachers (a higher
reality, transcendent existence) themselves

bleakly sheepish and short-lived. Soul went
and simile (discredited, lesser species

of dissembling) and subjunctives hung
back and world was ours a moment without

compromise, for the asking for the taking seriously.

◻ ◻ ◻

Plainly what we take into the world
such as the basket she carries

for her sheet music, books to go
back to the library, Italian crackers

from the organic grocery
the supermarket doesn't carry.

With her fine insouciance
but awkwardly too, the big nest-like

basket not best for books which sit aslant
on their corners. So what we've shaped

imperfectly to our uses, the cedar beam
cut a little long we bang into place

to support the old wisteria we can't lift
the whole of up to, so cut some away.

And what just comes, becoming
miraculously ours, sunlight we have

to walk into on the winter moss
at one with thought or thoughtlessness.

And something sullen at the guessed
extremities, a guest if welcomed in

seated at the long pine table
speaking its mind.

❏ ❏ ❏

First person singular/first
person universal of the new intimacy

the I (or i, embarrassed to be thought
imperious, self-serving) misunderstood

as confessional (a serf of the old order—
obsequious, regretful, guilty) sang self

resplendent in context, as difficult as
the physical is defining, constraining

body. Who remembers? Too few knew
its reward, responsibility, before the slack-

assed sentimentalists bestowed
esteem as birthright, community

upon any association. Evolving here
the missing persons community:

web-footed new age old souls surfing
Facebook. Friending. Tweeting. And here flits

the avatar over all, the You made from choices
of weaponry, loincloth, eye-colour, logo

bought on-line. The firm tits or six-pack
are Its, and the easy lay in the easy

lie of lazy desire gone sacred. It'll fuck
off and die at the time appointed

in the appointed manner and somewhere
digital points accrued will be forever

its totality. Number them you who
would exceed it. It numbers you.

❑ ❑ ❑

No-one else's stuff mixed in
with your precious possessions . . .

—moving company TV commercial

Everything fits in the stall
or the climatized container. The boat

out of the wind, Dad's guns leaning.
Mum's sideboard. My generation's

sidebar: all we won't let go of
or what won't go into the basement

or there is no basement to the condo.
No Freudian crawlspace, Perls in the attic.

A Salvation Army memorial salver tarnished
in a corner, salvage. I drive by daily, dream leaving

behind a houseful. Lock and leave. The old best
modernist materialists too: Williams, Berry, Oppen—

in boxes in the new library, clear heads in the *cloud*
of an *actual* world gone googley, babyish. Back

in slow. Everything fits in the stall
there, mid-air of our understanding, choke

then urgent click and stutter
of the starter motor. Closer. Careful

opening the big doors. Precarious tilt

of our stacked particulars. Our very own info
condensing into words, made things/of

things made, might make a home. Things
we can hardly say, can't read now, can't live

with but keep on buying, hoarding, ignoring . . .
are relics of a lost chance, a plausible religion.

❑ ❑ ❑

. . . What is inexplicable

Is the "preponderance of objects."
                              —George Oppen

Never to be numbered as each
is divisible into further singularities unto infinity.

So let not the poverty of my meagre best attention
diminish my singing their celebration; whether

in adversity the five robins suddenly
on the lawn peck and pull

in any respect as grief does or despair at me, or love
they are there and worthy. Now they are more.

Whether the grain of the sill is expressed
in the retraction of my fingers across it, in the idle

flexing of my hand, the window allows me
a frame of the foggy morning, the inexplicable

preponderance peopled with objects, subject
to any taxonomy of whim. I am always unprepared

for them and that is their relative freedom, mine. So let
proximity determine and know us as it does. Let

me learn all over again how each thing, anything newly
considered is dignified. All things considered there

is no other way. Let their qualities shape
my senses as my senses shape me and the space

we share inversely be inhabited—not lonely, wild
with fancy and sentiment, projection, terror. Let wild

space be the preponderance it is of the possibility
of me within as my explorations enlarge and down-

shift and humble. Let it forever be too
big for me in the ways it is infinite

that I might in my days have room to be new
outside the dark boxes and the manipulations

of the light boxes where we have determined
all and revel in our artifice, and half-believe we live.

❏ ❏ ❏

So much depends upon . . .

                   —William Carlos Williams

In Giotto's *Last Judgement*, as
in all art that lasts, judgement is

suspended. Though the damned are damned
and demons twist in their guts and genitals end-

lessly and without end the saved are saved and arrayed
in rank as apostles, saints, clergy and penitent

usurers should be, those top-shelf angels working
the blue vault's pulleys and curtains have yet to reveal

new heaven and earth beneath the sun and the moon.
Even the dead emerge in neutral, indeterminate hue, neither

cadaverous, nor as babes, nor aged. They are more restored
than resurrected, returned in their prime to their prime

anxieties, comforts. Bland and chubby and waist-
deep still in crevasses of stylized stone or ice most

turn in prayer to the Saviour. As if all will be asked
of them again: joy and suffering, a further test

of the will. We know the one helping another
into the picture, and the one who slips forward coming

out, and that only compassion and clumsiness inhibit
their return to worship, to the status quo. But here is one

might go the distance the masterpiece lasts and beyond.
He is all wrong, and clambers up, turned about, from a coffin

the blue of a toy-box. A grimace
and squint of consternation enlivens

his effort. He could be shortsighted, wilfully
obstinate, even stupid, but I take his concentration up-

on the composition's lower left-hand corner to be
serious and extendable. What of the fictive marble motif

of painted border? What of the salt-leaching stone beneath
the fresco's lustrous skin, and the unconditioned air

outdoors, alive with showers and traffic splashing
where we an hour ago these

centuries later came in? To him, to us, to
renaissance plus the unhinged exit

doors sigh open: contingency. It's enough.

Laszlo Loves Erasure

Laszlo wants an elephant
and Mum does one, a few deft

strokes with the special pencil
on his magic tablet and bang

it's gone as he hits the slide knob over
and back and clears the slate for

circles, circles, wonderful
circles for one so young and bang

so vehement and decisive as once we
hit the chrome levers, the carriage returns

on those behemoth typewriters when the fit
was on us like reloading a gun and bang

Laszlo wants an elephant.

Finally

Finally, will
art save your life?

Love? Knowledge?
Only nothing

is immense and momentous and unmade

enough. Fill your life
as you will you will

go singly all the way to empty, the full peace
that returns every piece and participle

of the world to the world.

That May Be

That May be the robins build
again beneath the eaves, chickadees
stuff the swallows' box with moss. A snake
deliberates across the wet patio seeking

worm or slug. That May be a sprig
of lilac exclaims above the pergola
and my look up is seconded
by heavy-headed cherry
blossom, shaded

jonquil, tulip,
rhododendron and
dogwood winking further
back in the forest. That May be all

accumulates in greens and birdsong
and rotten lumber on the lawn from
the old deck torn apart, for rebuilding.
That May be she'll walk the length of the new

boards to the white lilac pulling a branch
to her face for its fragrance or perchance her
pretty hand stray playfully under

my waistband; maybe that's all
one needs to begin again (that and taking

a Himalayan blue poppy or rufous
hummingbird to the eye) but I
say it too, or it says

me, the phrase unbidden that may be
wish, permission, equivocation, but firstly
is the little start I'm given, giving, that May be.

NOTES & ACKNOWLEDGEMENTS

Thanks to the editors of the following publications where some of these poems first appeared:

The Capilano Review
The Fiddlehead
Grain
Lake
The Malahat Review
Parliamentary Poet Laureate website
Prism
Rocksalt
The Walrus

The Ronsard translation, "Beauty becoming . . .", was first published in the broadsheet series, *Under Strange Sail*, Barbarian Press, Mission, 2007.

"Pin-holes" was privately printed by the poet at High Ground in celebration of his 60th birthday.

"En Route" was first published as a companion piece broadsheet to the D. C. Scott poem of the same title in *The Companions Series*, High Ground Press, Madeira Park, 2009.

Thanks to Ursula Vaira at Leaf Press for the chapbook, *Self Storage*.

The Ezra Pound lines are from Canto XVII, *Selected Poems of Ezra Pound* (p.120), New Directions, New York, 1957

The Mahmoud Darwish lines are from *The Butterfly's Burden* (p. 19), Copper Canyon Press, Port Townsend, 2007.

"En Route" by Duncan Campbell Scott is from *The Oxford Book of Canadian Verse*, Oxford University Press, Toronto, 1970.

The Lew Welch lines are from *Ring of Bone* (p. v), Grey Fox Press, Bolinas, 1973.

"Anthem" is a "translation" (from Beetle into English) of transcription #23-3, notebook 6, May 23, *2001 Tunnel Mountain*, by Ernie Kroeger. Kroeger's transcriptions are rubbings of bark beetle engravings created in the phloem layer of lodgepole pines.

The Ronsard lines are from *Les Amours, Matisse – Ronsard* (p. 6), Les Peintres Du Livre, Paris, 1970.

The Geoffrey Hill lines are from *Tenebrae* (p. 19), André Deutsch, London, 1978.

Thanks to artist Paul Feiler and the Redfern Gallery for permission to reproduce *Janicon LXXXIX* on the cover of this work. The catalogue referred to in the poem "Janicon" is *Paul Feiler: The Near and the Far*, Tate St Ives, 2005.

Thanks to Sharon Thesen for the term "aboutist" ("Around & Aboutist"): "Although I am an 'aboutist' (i.e. I believe in content), or 'Aboutiste du Nord,' I have a sort of aversion to writing 'about' nature." Quoted from conversations with Nancy Holmes in poetics.ca #5, summer 2005.

Thanks to the Canada Council for the Arts for assistance to the poet in the writing of this book.

KEITH SHAW

Published widely in Canada, John Pass's poetry has also appeared in the US, the UK and Ireland. His most recent books, comprising the quartet *AT LARGE*, are *The Hour's Acropolis* (Harbour), *Radical Innocence* (Harbour), *Water Stair* (Oolichan)—shortlisted for the Governor General's Award—and *Stumbling in the Bloom* (Oolichan)—winner of the Governor General's Award. John Pass lives with his wife, writer Theresa Kishkan, on BC's Sunshine Coast.